The Electoral College

The Electoral College

Suzanne LeVert

Watts LIBRARY™

Franklin Watts
A Division of Scholastic Inc.
New York • Toronto • London • Auckland • Sydney
Mexico City • New Delhi • Hong Kong
Danbury, Connecticut

Note to readers: Definitions for words in **bold** can be found in the Glossary at the back of this book.

The illustration on the cover shows an elector in Massachusetts dropping his vote in the ballot box. The photograph opposite the title page shows electors voting.

Library of Congress Cataloging-in-Publication Data

LeVert, Suzanne.
    The Electoral college / Suzanne LeVert.
        p. cm. — (Watts library)
    Published simultaneously in Canada.
    Includes bibliographical references and index.
    ISBN 0-531-12292-1 (lib. bdg.)   0-531-16606-6 (pbk.)
    1. Electoral college—United States—Juvenile literature. 2. Presidents—United States—Election—Juvenile literature. 3. United States—Politics and government—Juvenile literature. I. Title. II. Series.
JK529.L48 2004
324.6'3—dc22

2004002006

Contents

The 2000 presidential candidates, Al Gore and George W. Bush, meet for a televised debate. In their race for the presidency, the two would end up fighting each other in court over legal issues involving voting procedures.

Chapter One

The 2000 Presidential Election

On November 7, 2000, election officials from all the states counted more than 101.5 million total votes cast for the two major United States presidential and vice presidential candidates. George W. Bush and Dick Cheney ran on the Republican **slate** and Albert A. Gore and Joseph Lieberman on the Democratic **ticket**. Most people who went to the polls that day thought that they voted directly for their candidates. If so, then the two people who received the most number of national **popular votes**, or votes cast by individual citizens in the country, would have won the election. In 2000, Al Gore received some 500,000 more popular votes than George W. Bush did. Yet on January 20, 2001, Inauguration Day, George W. Bush became the forty-third president of the United States.

Many Americans were confused by the outcome of the 2000 election. Why didn't the candidate with the most votes win? How did this happen? The answer is spelled out in the **U.S. Constitution**, the document that created our government and its rules and procedures. The Constitution also lays out the system for electing presidents and vice presidents. This system is called the **Electoral College**. It has been revised over the years through federal laws and changes called constitutional **amendments**.

The Electoral College Decides

The Electoral College is a system made up of a group, or college, of people called **electors**. Officials from the various **political parties** in each state pick their electors before the presidential election. Electors pledge to support their party's presidential candidates for president and vice president. When citizens make their choice on Election Day, they are voting for the electors of their candidates for president and vice president, not directly for each candidate. The state's winning

The U.S. Constitution was drawn up in Philadelphia in 1787 by fifty-five **delegates** of the original thirteen colonies at a meeting called the **Constitutional Convention**. The Constitution created our form of government. It is considered the supreme law of the country, and all federal, state, local, and other laws and constitutions must be in agreement with its rules and principles.

As part of his role as vice president, Al Gore served as president of the Senate. The president of the Senate certifies the electoral votes.

electors are the electors whose candidates win their state's popular vote. In December, after the election, the winning electors in the fifty states and the District of Columbia meet in their state capitals to officially cast their state's electoral votes. Their votes are sent to state and federal officials. At a special meeting of **Congress**, the electoral votes from all the states are read and counted. The candidates for president and for vice president with the most electoral votes from all the states are then officially declared the winners of the presidential election.

Every state has a certain number of electoral votes. The number depends upon the state's population. In 2000, there were a total of 538 electoral votes among all the states. In order to win the presidency, a candidate must win a majority (at least one more than half of the total) or 270 electoral votes. It doesn't matter who has the most popular votes in the country. What matters is who has the most electoral votes tallied, or added up, from each of the states. The candidate who wins the greatest number of national popular votes almost always wins the most electoral votes as well. There have been only four U.S. presidential elections that did not turn out this way. The presidential election of 2000 was the only one of these occurred that in the last century.

Too Close to Call

The Bush-Gore contest was one of the closest presidential elections in U.S. history. On election night, Gore was ahead in popular votes, with Bush leading by a small number of electoral votes. In the end, the final decision depended on Florida, the last state to count its votes. Whoever won the most votes in Florida would win its twenty-five electoral votes. Those votes would give that candidate a majority of electoral votes in the country. Deciding the winner of Florida's election and the winner of the presidency turned out to be more difficult than anyone had imagined. In fact, it would take thirty-six days to decide who won the most votes in Florida.

When the votes in Florida were added up, the results were so close that that there was an automatic statewide recount of votes. The voting machine recount showed George Bush ahead by only 327 out of six million votes cast!

The stakes were very high. The next U.S. president would be the person who won Florida's electoral votes. The Democ-

10

People spent hours reviewing and recounting ballots in Florida.

ratic Party requested manual recounts, or counting by people, in four counties. They felt that people would be more accurate examiners than machines. The next day, Republican Party officials went to the Florida federal court to stop manual recounts. They argued that they were unnecessary and unfair. This was only the beginning of weeks of court hearings, with the Democrats arguing in favor of recounting votes and the Republicans arguing against. Some counties started recounting even as the political parties took their cases to the courts. The inspectors looked at every one of the voters' **ballots** to make sure that their vote was recorded correctly.

In counties that went forward with manual recounts, inspectors from both parties teamed up to examine the punch cards. Looking carefully at cards that were damaged or not clearly

The Truth About Chads

There were many problems with the voting process in Florida. In several counties, voters had trouble understanding the instructions on the ballot. Some were afraid they had not voted for the candidate they had wanted. Others thought they had voted twice by mistake. In some counties in Florida and other states, voters use punch cards to make their choices, a method that often causes machine errors. In Florida, about 10,000 ballots were thrown out, for instance, because they had no punch marks at all. In other instances, cards had two marks or just slight indentations or dimples. Many cards were not punched through all the way, leaving a square piece of paper called a **chad** dangling in any number of directions from the card.

marked, the teams did their best to figure out which candidates the voter chose. They also had to decide whether their vote should be counted or rejected if the mark was not clear. There were few set rules to guide the inspectors' decisions. Some counties counted dimpled cards, while others did not. Republicans argued that this was not a fair way to count votes. The courts did not agree. In fact the Florida Supreme Court ordered that the manual recounts continue. The Republican legal team decided to take their arguments right to the top. They filed a suit in the U.S. Supreme Court to stop all recounts in Florida.

Supreme Decision

On December 9, 2000, more than a month after Election Day, George W. Bush's lawyers brought his case to the Supreme Court in Washington, D.C. In the court case *Bush* v. *Gore*, the Bush team argued that Florida should stop the recount and the Gore team argued to continue the process. Some people thought the Florida courts should decide the issue because the Constitution gives states the responsibility for settling election disputes.

The Supreme Court, however, did hear the case. On December 12, 2000, it ruled to end the recount in Florida. Defeated by the nation's highest court and with Bush ahead by a few hundred votes at the last count, Al Gore ended his fight the next day. George W. Bush won the electoral votes needed and became the forty-third president in 2001.

The 2000 election started many debates about presidential election rules. Why is there an Electoral College? What were the designers or **framers of the Constitution** thinking when they devised this way of electing our presidents? Let's explore some of the ideas that led the framers to create this system when they wrote the U.S. Constitution.

The Highest Court in the Land

The U.S. Supreme Court is made up of nine judges, who are appointed by presidents and serve on the Court for life. It is the highest court in the United States. The Court can overturn decisions and laws of any federal court in the country, as well as any in the fifty states' supreme courts.

Protesters clashed outside the U.S. Supreme Court building as the Court considers whether to allow the recounts in Florida to continue.

James Madison and other delegates at the Constitutional Convention worked on creating a new type of government.

Chapter Two

The Constitutional Foundation

"If men were angels, no government would be necessary," stated James Madison. Called the father of the Constitution, Madison was a state **legislator** from Virginia who played a leading role at the Constitutional Convention, in 1787. He was deeply committed to unifying the thirteen states under one system of laws and protections. He became the fourth president, serving two terms beginning in 1809.

Time for a Change

At the convention, James Madison and his fellow delegates agreed that a strong national government would provide unity and protect the people and the states. The newly independent and expanding nation needed a central, or federal, structure to unify the states, coin money, raise taxes for services, command an army, and create laws that applied to all citizens in all states. At that time, the national government consisted only of a small congress, with little power to make decisions. Each state had its own laws, even its own form of money. It was time for a big change.

A Government Is Born

Having only recently won independence from a country ruled by a king, the framers were cautious about giving too much power to one person or political body. Through the Constitution, they set up a **federal republic**. This system balances the power of the federal government with respect for states' rights. It includes three branches of government at the national level. Each branch keeps an eye on, or "checks," the others' actions. They include the executive branch, the judicial branch, and the legislative branch. No branch can make a policy or pass a law without the approval of one or both of the other branches. States have their own governments, including local and statewide **legislatures** and court systems with similar checks and balances. State courts, for example, must review the laws that state legislators pass.

Two Houses of Congress

The Constitution established a **bicameral** Congress, made up of two houses, or chambers, called the Senate and the House of Representatives. Each state elects two senators. Until 1913, state governments selected their senators, but today citizens elect their two senators in statewide elections. Each state also elects a number of representatives that is related to its population. The more people living in a state, the more representatives they can elect to the House of Representatives. Voters select their representatives through elections held in different areas or districts of each state. Every ten years the residents of all states are counted in a national **census** to see if the population has changed. If it has, the number of representatives to the House and the number of electoral votes could change.

Representation and Slavery

The issue of slavery divided the country from its very beginning and affected the crafting of the Constitution. Some delegates wanted to end slavery altogether and others wanted to continue the practice. The framers compromised on this issue. They decided that Congress would not interfere with the slave trade for twenty years. They allowed slave-owning states to count people held in slavery in their census, which increased their representation in Congress and the number of their electoral votes. States, however, could count slaves as only three-fifths of a whole person. Slaves could be counted, but could not vote. It would be nearly a century before the practice of slavery was abolished and people held in slavery were freed and recognized as full citizens.

Electing a President

Another important issue at the convention was whether an individual or a group of people should head the executive branch. Once they decided on having one leader, the delegates had to figure out how this individual would be selected. One idea was for Congress to make the choice. Another proposal was for state governments to decide. Some delegates suggested that the citizens of the United States vote in a national election. Then the person with the most popular votes would become president. The framers rejected this idea as well. Many feared that ordinary people would not have enough knowledge or education to make wise and informed choices. Voters might choose candidates only from their own states. Candidates from states with large populations would have a big advantage over smaller states. The framers wanted to

make sure that all states, large and small, had a say in selecting the president.

The College of Electors

The framers opted for an election system first called the College of Electors. The college, which means a selected group, the delegates thought, would be made up of distinguished and educated people chosen by each state. They would, in turn, select the president and vice president. The system is outlined in Article II, section 1 of the Constitution. Each state had a number of electors (and electoral votes) equal to its number of senators and representatives in Congress. States would decide

At the Constitutional Convention, the framers decided that the executive branch should be headed by one leader. They wrestled with how to create the best election system.

The Federalists, the First Political Party

At the time the Constitution was written, formal political parties did not exist. There were, however, two groups with different opinions about the nation's new government. The Federalists supported a strong central government. Headed by Alexander Hamilton, the group voiced their opinions in a series of articles called *The Federalist Papers.*

The Anti-Federalists favored stronger states' rights. During the first two elections, these groups rallied to support the candidates who favored their point of view. In the early 1800s formal political parties were formed and their numbers grew quickly. Today, there are more than fifty-five different political parties in the United States.

their own election methods and selection of their electors. Members of Congress and employees of the federal government were not allowed to serve as electors. So far, all of these rules remain in effect today.

This original version, however, called for electors to cast two votes for president. At least, one of the votes had to be for a candidate outside their home states. The person with the majority of electoral votes tallied from all the states would become president. The candidate with the next greatest number of electoral votes became vice president. If no one obtained a majority of votes or if there were a tie, the House would choose the president from among the top five contenders. Representatives would break into groups according to their home states, and each state group was to have one vote. The candidate who received a majority of votes in the House would become president. If none of the runners-up won a majority of votes, or if there were a tie, the House would decide the winner from the five candidates with the most votes. The candidate with the second highest number of votes would become vice president. In case of two or more remaining candidates having the same number of votes, the vice president would be chosen by the Senate.

In 1788, the required number of states (nine) ratified, or approved, the Constitution. The first task in forming the new government was to select the nation's first president. Remember, there were no formal political parties and candidates did not campaign for office at that time. State legislatures chose electors in most states. In 1789, twelve candidates were in the running for the presidency. George Washington was the clear choice for president, and he won the office easily with sixty-nine of a total of 138 electoral votes cast. John Adams came in second and became the first vice president. Not all elections would go so smoothly. As the country grew and political parties evolved in the 1800s, the Electoral College would need some additional adjustments.

George Washington won the first election with sixty-nine electoral votes.

After Thomas Jefferson received the same number of electoral votes as Aaron Burr, House of Representatives voted to determine the winner of the 1800 presidential election. They selected Jefferson to be the president.

Chapter Three

Disputes and Changes

In 1800, the Federalist Party supported President John Adams for reelection, as well as candidates Charles Pinckney and John Jay. The newly formed Democratic-Republican Party favored Thomas Jefferson and Aaron Burr.

The Federalist electors split their votes among Adams and the other candidates, while the Democratic-Republican electors chose Jefferson and Burr. The electoral votes showed that Jefferson and Burr won the majority of the electors' votes, but they each won the same number. Each received 73 votes out of 138. In the case of a tie, the Constitution requires the House of Representatives to decide the outcome.

At the time, most House representatives belonged to the Federalist Party. They had to choose between two candidates from the opposing Democratic-Republican Party. After thirty-six tries, House members finally gave Jefferson a majority of their votes. He became the third U.S. president, and Burr became his vice president.

Changing the Rules

After the election of 1800, Congress changed electoral voting procedures to help avoid such tied electoral votes. The Twelfth Amendment, passed by Congress in 1804, requires each elector to cast one vote for president and a separate vote for vice president. The rule that they could choose only one candidate from their home state remained in effect. The amendment also states that if no one receives a majority of

So You Want to Be President?

In order to become president of the United States, a person must be at least thirty-five years old and born in the United States. Presidents serve for four years and only can run once for reelection. The president makes sure that the nation's laws are carried out and is the chief commander of the U.S. military. Presidents also appoint judges to the Supreme Court and officials to federal agencies and departments. As head of state, he or she works with other world leaders in dealing with foreign affairs.

In Washington, D.C. (shown here), politicians sought to make changes to the Electoral College after the 1800 presidential election.

electoral votes for president, then the House selects the president from among the top three contenders. If no one receives a majority of votes for vice president, then the Senate selects the vice president from among the top two contenders for that office.

By the early 1800s, most states chose their electors by popular vote, ballots cast by the states' eligible voters. During this time, political parties grew in number and in power. Parties organized political campaigns to gain public support for their candidates. Supporters created posters, songs, buttons, and slogans. They also organized parades and marches. By the late

1800s the candidates themselves took to the road to meet voters and make speeches.

The role of the elector changed as well. Electors were selected by political parties and were expected to support their party's candidates if they won the most votes in their state. Their job rapidly became one of agreeing with or "rubber-stamping" the results of their state's popular election. To date, only four winning presidents won a majority of electoral votes but lost the total popular votes in the country. And in only two elections in U.S. history, the elections of 1800 and 1824, the House of Representatives decided the winner. The Electoral College is not a perfect system, as several close and unusual U.S. presidential elections show.

Unexpected Results and Controversies

In the election of 1824, Andrew Jackson received roughly 38,000 more popular votes and more electoral votes than the three other top contenders, John Quincy Adams, William Crawford, and Henry Clay. All four candidates were from the Democratic-Republican Party, but none of them received a majority of electoral votes. For the second time, and so far the last time, the House had to choose.

In a close vote, the House picked John Quincy Adams over Andrew Jackson for president. Jackson and others believed that since Jackson won more popular votes than the other candidates and none of them won a majority of electoral votes,

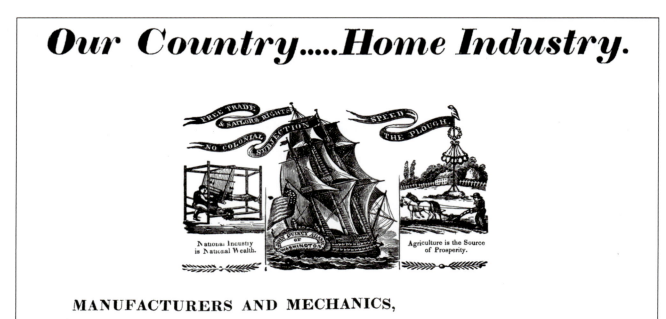

Our Country.....Home Industry.

FREE TRADE & SAILORS RIGHTS

NO COLONIAL SUBJECTION

SPEED THE PLOUGH

National Industry is National Wealth.

JOHN QUINCY ADAMS OF WASHINGTON

Agriculture is the Source of Prosperity.

MANUFACTURERS AND MECHANICS,

Your enemies have rallied under the banner of Gen. Jackson—the same man whom they a few days since declared a tyrant and a murderer. One of their avowed objects is a repeal of all the laws which have been enacted for the encouragement of manufactures.

If the Jackson Party prevail, a majority of the next Congress will be opposed to the tariff, to mechanics, manufacturers, and domestic industry. As proof of this, the Jackson papers, nearly

votes that you are not the dupes of such men as Coleman, who has always been your enemy. He tells you to vote for General Jackson: vote directly opposite to his advice, and you will vote for your country. As a proof of this, I ask who has always sided with the British against his country? Will you not answer, Coleman? Who has abused the best patriots America ever produced? Is not Wm. Coleman the man? Who scandalized Madison? Who vilified Jefferson? Who has slandered Henry Clay?

he was clearly the people's choice. With citizens in all but six states by then voting for their party's electors, this was the first time the popular vote had real weight. Unfortunately for Jackson, the popular vote did not win over the members of the House of Representatives.

This is a campaign ad for John Quincy Adams, which attacks Andrew Jackson.

The Disputed Election of 1876

Yet another test of the Electoral College system occurred after the 1876 election, often called the "disputed" election. The two major political parties were the Republican Party and the Democratic Party, as they are today. The Democrats

An Unusual Election

The election of 1836 produced no vice presidential candidate with a majority of electoral votes. For the first and only time in U.S. history, the Senate had to decide. The votes went to Richard Johnson, who became vice president under President Martin Van Buren.

nominated Governor Samuel J. Tilden of New York and Thomas Hendricks of Indiana for president and vice president. The Republicans selected Governor Rutherford B. Hayes of Ohio and William Wheeler of New York. A number of other, smaller parties had developed by this time and candidates from the Prohibition, Greenback, American-National, and other parties also entered the race.

Tilden beat Hayes in popular votes by about 264,000 and received 184 electoral votes. Hayes received 165 electoral votes. The winner needed 185 electoral votes to have a majority. Tilden was short only one vote! There were an additional twenty electoral votes in question and not yet counted. Three

This illustration shows Senator Ferry announcing the results of the 1876 presidential election. Although Governor Samuel J. Tilden won the popular vote, Rutherford B. Hayes ended up the most electoral votes.

Denied the Right to Vote

During the early history of the United States, many states restricted voting rights to landowners, while others allowed only white men over the age of twenty-one to vote. Some states barred Catholics and non-Christians from voting. No state allowed African-Americans, free or held in slavery, to vote. In 1870, the Fifteenth Amendment to the U.S. Constitution ruled that citizens could not be denied the right to vote because of their race, color, or past slavery. Women in many states could not vote until Congress passed the Nineteenth Amendment in 1920. In 1924, Congress extended citizenship rights, including the right to vote, to American Indians. Some states, however, barred American Indians from voting. Today all citizens eighteen years or older have the right to vote with only a few exceptions.

southern states had sent two sets of electoral votes, one set for Tilden and one for Hayes. One vote from Oregon was challenged because of an issue about one of its electors. Congress created a commission to review the disputed electoral votes. The majority of the fifteen commission members were Republicans, and they cast their votes for Hayes. Just two days before the new president should take office, the commission awarded all of the disputed votes to Hayes. Hayes, not Tilden, won the election by one vote and became the nineteenth U.S. president.

To avoid disputes about states' electoral votes in the future, Congress passed The Electoral Count Act in 1887. It gives states the responsibility to settle elector and electoral vote disputes before sending their votes to Congress. The law also changed the date that electors would meet to cast their votes from December to January to give more states time to settle any disagreements before sending their votes to Congress. This would be changed back to December again in 1934.

The Tight Race of 1888

In 1888, President Grover Cleveland, a Democrat, won the popular vote in his bid for reelection by about 100,000 votes out of a total of 11 million. His opponent, Benjamin Harrison, however, won sixty-five more electoral votes than Cleveland. Harrison received more electoral votes by winning the popular vote in thirty-two states, giving him all those states' electoral votes. Cleveland had received more popular votes, but mostly from six large southern states. This election showed how the Electoral College can give all states, no matter how small, a voice in electing our presidents. It also encouraged candidates to appeal to voters from states of all sizes and regions of the country. At the same time, the election led to

Changes through the Years

Two constitutional amendments and a number of state and federal laws have changed the original version of the Electoral College system. In addition to those already mentioned:

- In 1845, Congress selected one day for all states to choose their electors: the Tuesday following the first Monday in November in years divisible by four. We call it Election Day.
- In 1934, Congress set the Monday after the second Wednesday in December as the day for electors to meet and cast their votes. And on January 6, Congress gathers to count the electoral votes and announce the winner.

increased campaign planning, with candidates deciding where they had the greatest support and which states might gain them the most electoral votes.

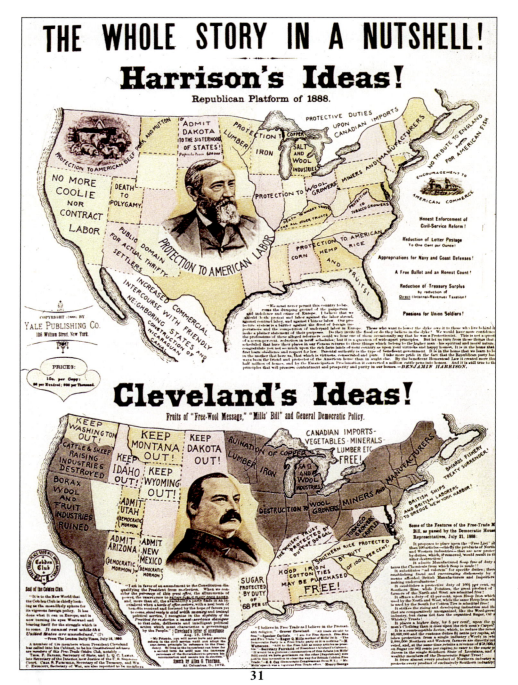

Created by the Republican Party, these two contrasting maps of the United States are meant to illustrate the different positions of Grover Cleveland and Benjamin Harrison, the two candidates of the 1888 presidential election, on tariff policies.

Electors in the Electoral College follow much the same process as was outlined by the Constitution.

Chapter Four

The Electoral College Today

With some changes along the way, the Electoral College the framers created is basically the same system used today to elect the president of the United States. This is quite astonishing as our country has grown and changed greatly in the past two centuries. Today, the United States has a population of about 249 million people in fifty states, and the District of Columbia, spread out over some 3.5 million square miles. People can communicate instantly with anyone in the world.

Modern technology provides news the moment it happens, and with colorful pictures. Quite a different landscape from the 1770s!

These and other huge changes in American life have had an impact on presidential elections. There are more than fifty-five major and smaller political parties in the United States today. In 2000, about fourteen different parties put forward candidates for president and vice president in various states.

Since the mid-1800s, though, the Democratic and Republican parties have been the main two parties in the nation. Every president since then has come from one or the other party. Today these two parties spend many millions of dollars during presidential campaigns for thousands of hours of television and other forms of advertising to convince voters of their candidates' qualities. This affected the role of electors as well.

Loyalty Counts

Today's electors are not, as the framers envisioned, isolated from political influence. They are selected by a specific political party and pledge their loyalty and support for their party's candidates.

Voters in each state now select a slate or group of electors. Although they are, indeed, real people, voters rarely know them or even their names. Most states' presidential ballots read "the electors for . . ." in front of the candidates' names. Although the framers thought electors should vote however they wished, today's electors are expected to vote for the

candidates of the party that selected them. If their party's ticket of candidates wins the popular vote in the state, the electors become the state's official electors. They will cast their state's electoral votes after the national election is over.

Twenty-six states require electors to vote according to political parties' wishes, but there are no penalties if they don't. In other states, electors are free to vote however they wish, but that happens very rarely. The winning electors almost always

This is an example of how a presidential ballot might look like.

cast their electoral votes for their party's candidates. An elector who votes for another party's candidate is called a "faithless elector."

The Details

The Democratic and Republican parties nominate their presidential candidates at their **national conventions**, usually held in the summer before the general election. State groups, or delegations, vote on their choice for nominee. The candidate with the majority of votes wins his or her party's nomination. The winning candidate selects a running mate, or candidate for vice president.

The parties select their electors before the election and send their names to their state's election official. On Election Day, voters in each state choose the slate of electors for the team they want to be president and vice president. The electors winning the most votes in the state are named as that state's electors. The exceptions to this are Maine and Nebraska. In these states, two electors are chosen by statewide popular vote, and the remainder are chosen by popular vote in the states' **congressional districts**.

State governments are expected to resolve any election disputes at least six days before their electors meet to cast their votes. After determining their slate of electors (for the candidates who won the popular vote) each state governor sends a certificate with the names and the numbers of votes of the state's appointed electors to the archivist of the United States. The governor then sends six duplicate certificates to the electors. On the Monday following the second Wednesday of December, the winning slates of electors meet in their state capitals and cast their votes, one for president and one for vice president.

On Election Day, citizens vote for electors, not just candidates.

The electors each make two lists of votes. One list is of their votes for president and the other contains their votes for vice president. They then attach these lists to the six certificates they had received from their state governors. The electors send two certificates to their state's secretary of state and one to the U.S. Senate. The day after their meeting, they send two certificates to the archivist and one to the judge of the district where they meet.

A group of electors cast their votes for president and vice president.

Home Sweet Home

The Constitution requires that electors cast at least one of their votes for a candidate outside their state. This means that the candidates for president and vice president running on the same ticket cannot live in the same state or they lose that state's electoral votes. Politicians sometimes have to think and act quickly to make sure they obey this rule. Vice President Dick Cheney, for instance, changed his residency from Texas to Wyoming four days before the Republican national convention. When Texas resident George W. Bush chose Cheney as his running mate, he did not violate the requirement that candidates on the same ticket be from different states. Cheney was no longer an official resident of Texas.

Deadlines, Deadlines

According to federal law, the president of the Senate (the vice president of the United States) should receive all the states' certificates of electoral votes by the fourth Wednesday in December. If for some reason they don't, the state's secretary of state sends the electors' certificates and asks the district court judge to do the same. So that is why the electors sent extra certificates to their secretary of state.

After an election, Congress meets for the first time in the new year on January 3. On this date, the U.S. archivist sends each of the two houses of Congress all the certificates received from the governors. That is why the archivist receives two certificates.

Congress meets again on January 6 (unless that date falls on a Sunday) in the House of Representatives to count the electoral votes. The Senate president opens and presents the certificates of every state's electoral votes in alphabetical order. Selected members of Congress called **tellers** read, record, and count the votes. Then, finally, the Senate president announces the candidates with the majority of electoral votes, the next president and vice president of the United States.

Members may challenge or object to a particular electoral vote. After each certificate is read, the Senate president "calls for objections, if any." Objections must be made in writing and signed by at least one member from the Senate and one from the House. If there is an objection, Senate and House members hold separate meetings to vote on the objection. A

The electors' votes, stored in boxes, are being taken to Congress.

majority of members in both houses must vote to reject the disputed electoral vote for it to be thrown out. Otherwise, it must be counted.

In the event that a candidate does not obtain a majority of

the electoral votes for president, the procedure outlined in the Twelfth Amendment is used. The House selects the president from the top three contenders. Each state has one vote, and a majority of all votes will decide the winner. When no candidate for vice president receives the necessary electoral votes, the Senate resolves the issue. The last time this happened was in 1836.

Today, the reading and tabulating of electoral votes in Congress is basically a ceremony that confirms the voting results from Election Day. At noon on January 20, the elected president and vice president are sworn into office.

The election process ends with the winning presidential candidate being sworn into office.

Senator Hillary Clinton is one of the many people who have expressed some concern about the Electoral College.

Chapter Five

Future of the College

In November 2000, newly elected Senator Hillary Rodham Clinton called for an end to the Electoral College. She stated, "I've always thought we had outlived the need for an Electoral College, and now that I am going to the Senate, I am going to try to do what I can to make clear that the popular vote, the will of the people, should be followed."

Senator Clinton was not the only person to voice a strong opinion about the Electoral College, and she certainly was not the first. The system has been the subject of discussions since it was created. There are many people who still believe this system is the best way to elect our presidents. There are others who feel strongly that it does not serve the needs of a modern, democratic nation. Some call for it to be thrown out, and others support changes.

Not Fair! Get Rid of It!

Opponents of the Electoral College point out that this system allows a candidate to win the national popular vote, but not the presidency. The most recent example, of course, is the 2000 election. Many people thought it was not right that a candidate could win more total votes in the country and not win the election. A system that ignores the total votes of the people is not fair or democratic, they say.

Some opponents of the system think it gives small states more influence than their population deserves. Wyoming, for example, has three electoral votes, each one representing 151,196 people. California, on the other hand, has 54 electoral votes, one for every 551,112 people. Opponents state that this means that Wyoming's electoral votes are actually worth or "weigh" four times those of California. Others disagree. They claim that the system gives more populated states, or states with large urban areas, an advantage because of the large numbers of electoral votes at stake. The winner-takes-all system encourages candidates to focus on the heavily populated states, hoping to gain the most votes.

Some people believe that the Electoral College should not be used anymore and think it would be better to have the popular vote decide the winner of the presidential election.

Many oppose the system because it prevents third-party candidates from winning elections. They favor a system that encourages different points of view and, through popular votes, can help give candidates from other political parties a chance. Others simply believe that a national vote is the fairest way to make sure that every person's vote counts and that the candidate winning the most votes in the country is elected president.

Some opponents of the Electoral College system favor abolishing it altogether and simply count the total popular votes in the country. This approach would involve a big change, requiring an amendment to the Constitution. There have been many attempts to do this, but none has succeeded

Former Senator Birch Bayh has been a strong advocate for direct elections.

Constitutional Amendments

Changing the Constitution requires great support from members of Congress and state governments. In order for an amendment to become law, both the Senate and the House of Representatives must agree by a two-thirds majority in each chamber, and state legislatures in three-fourths of the states must approve the amendment. Although it has never been done, states can pass an amendment without approval from Congress. First, delegates from the interested states meet and agree on a proposed amendment. Their proposal is then taken back to their states for approval. The first phase of the process is to get two-thirds of all states to approve the amendment. The second step is to obtain the approval of three-fourths of all the states, which is the same tough requirement for all amendments that Congress proposes.

thus far. In fact, there have been about five hundred amendment proposals to change the Electoral College presented to Congress. Many have been approved by the House, but have failed to win enough support in the Senate.

Former Senator Birch Bayh of Indiana has introduced several bills calling for a constitutional amendment that would institute direct elections of the president and vice president. The ticket with the most votes, by at least 40 percent, would be the winner. His proposal also provides for a "runoff" election in case no one ticket receives 40 percent or more of the popular vote. The second round of the election, then, would be between the two top winning tickets. Although this proposal has not received enough support in Congress to go forward, it is one of the more common plans for revising our presidential elections.

Keep It! It Works!

On the other side are those who want to keep the Electoral College system in place. They believe it has served the country very well. With only a few exceptions, the candidates who received the most votes nationally have also won the most electoral votes. It is, they say, part of our federal system of government, which supports states' rights. In 1956 Senator John F. Kennedy said, "It is not only the unit vote for the Presidency we are talking about, but a whole solar system of governmental power. If it is proposed to change the balance of power of one of the elements of the system, it is necessary to consider the others."

Supporters say that every vote does count—in the state where it is cast. They point out that actually there is not one big election in November, but fifty-one separate elections. They take place in each of the fifty states and in the District of Columbia. The system helps ensure that the person elected has support from many states, not just the largest states or states in one region of the country. Candidates need all the electoral votes they can get, not just the largest number of popular votes in the country.

Keep It, but Change It!

One suggestion is to keep the Electoral College in place, but do away with individual electors. Because the state's electors almost always cast their votes for their party's winning candidates, they no longer serve any purpose. Another idea is to keep individual electors in each state, but require them to vote for their party's candidates or face a penalty. This idea would eliminate the possibility of votes from faithless electors. Either of these plans would require a constitutional amendment.

Others suggest that the winner-take-all method be replaced with a proportional plan. Electoral votes in a state would be related to the number of votes the candidates receive. A candidate might, for example, receive one electoral vote for every 10,000 votes received. The proportional plan would give candidates from all parties a chance of winning some electoral votes in each state. Candidates, then, would not "give up" on states where their party usually has little support because they actually could receive some electoral votes. This method could be put into effect throughout the country by means of a constitutional amendment. But because the Constitution gives states the right to decide how their electors are chosen, individual states could adopt this system by changing their state election laws.

Yet another suggestion is to choose electors by a combination of state and district-based voting within the state. Maine and Nebraska already use a form of this system. Two of their electoral votes go to the statewide winner. They distribute the remaining votes among the winners in congressional districts. This plan would require a change in state law rather than a constitutional amendment.

Does the Electoral College Have a Future?

According to the Gallup **poll** taken in 2000, about 61 percent of Americans asked said they favor abolishing the Electoral College, while 35 percent voted to keep the system as it is. Others were undecided. What do you think? Do you have ideas for a different system? Or do you think the Constitution created a good system? You can let your views be heard by writing to your U.S. representative or senator.

The plans and suggestions described in this chapter are just a few of the many proposals put forth by politicians, historians, political analysts, and others in recent years. The discussions and proposals for change will certainly continue. And should the United States experience yet another controversial election, the Electoral College's future will once again be the topic of national debates.

Surveys have been done to discover how citizens of the United States feel about the voting process and the Electoral College.

Timeline

1787	Delegates to the Constitutional Convention meet to write the U.S. Constitution, creating our federal government and establishing a Board of Electors to decide presidential elections. We now use the term Electoral College.
1788	A majority of states ratifies the Constitution. George Washington and John Adams receive the necessary electoral votes to become president and vice president, respectively.
1800	Thomas Jefferson wins the presidential election, but only after the House breaks a tie of electoral votes (73 to 73) between Jefferson and Aaron Burr. According to the rules then, Aaron Burr, with the next highest electoral votes, wins the office of vice president.
1804	States ratify the Twelfth Amendment, which states that electors will cast one vote for president and one vote for vice president.
1824	The House of Representatives elects John Quincy Adams president when no one presidential candidate receives a majority of electoral votes.
1836	The Senate elects Richard Johnson as vice president after Johnson fails to win the necessary majority of the Electoral College votes.
1872	Presidential candidate Horace Greeley dies between Election Day and the meeting of the Electoral College, but still receives three votes from the electors.
1876	Rutherford B. Hayes is elected president after failing to receive the majority of the popular vote. Disputed electoral votes from several states lead to the establishment of a special commission. The commission awards the disputed votes to Hayes, giving him the necessary number of electoral votes to become president.

continued on next page

1887	Congress enacts legislation giving the states final authority in deciding the legality of its choice of electors. The legislation also requires that both houses of Congress reach majority decisions when voting to reject a disputed electoral vote.
1888	Benjamin Harrison is elected president, losing the popular vote but winning the majority of electoral votes.
1961	The Twenty-Third Amendment passes, giving Washington, D.C., the same number of electors as the smallest state.
2000	The presidential election hinges on the popular vote in Florida and is finally decided on December 12, 2000. George W. Bush receives Florida's electoral votes and wins the election when the U.S. Supreme Court halts the recounts in that state.

Glossary

amendment—a change or revision. The U.S. Constitution has been amended twenty-seven times since it was created.

American Revolution—the fight for independence from England waged by the original thirteen colonies, which began in 1775

ballot—a sheet of paper listing candidates for political office on which a voter makes marks to cast his vote in favor of one or more of those candidates

bicameral—consisting of two houses, branches, or chambers. The Congress is a bicameral body, made up of the House of Representatives and the Senate.

census—a count of the number of people living in a country. In the United States, the census takes place every ten years, as required by the Constitution.

chad—a square piece of paper that remains on or hangs from a punch card ballot. Voting machines can produce a number of different types of chads, including hanging-door, swinging, dimpled, and other types.

congressional district—an area or part of a state divided for the purpose of voting for representatives of the House of Representatives. Each district is determined by the number of people living there and elects one person to the House.

Congress—the legislative branch of the U.S. government. It is made up of two parts, the Senate and the House of Representatives.

Constitutional Convention—a meeting of state delegates in Philadelphia, Pennsylvania, in 1787. The delegates drafted the U.S. Constitution at the convention.

delegate—a person chosen to represent a political party or an organization at a meeting or convention

Electoral College—the system of electing U.S. presidents and vice presidents. Each state has a certain number of votes, depending on its population. Washington, D.C., has three votes. In order to become president, a candidate must win a majority of these votes, or 270.

elector—a representative selected by a political party and chosen by his or her state's voters to elect the president and vice president

federal republic—the form of government created by the U.S. Constitution. It consists of three branches of government. The executive branch includes the president, vice president, and various federal departments. It carries out the country's laws. The legislative branch includes Congress, made up of the House of Representatives and the Senate. It makes the country's laws. The judicial branch consists of the Supreme Court and the federal courts. It checks laws to make sure they are in line with the Constitution.

framers of the Constitution—the fifty-five delegates to the Constitutional Convention who wrote the U.S. Constitution in 1787

legislator—an elected official of a local, state, or national legislature, or law-making body

legislature—a local, state, or national assembly charged with making laws

national conventions—meetings of delegates from all the states who represent the political parties. They gather during a presidential election year to help decide their party's position on various issues and to nominate the individuals who will run for president and vice president for their political party.

political party—a group made up of people who share the same viewpoints about laws and government. The two major political parties in the United States are the Democratic and the Republican Party.

poll—a tally of people's opinions conducted by a political party or by a private organization

popular vote—the total votes cast by individual voters for candidates in an election

slate—a list of candidates proposed for nomination or election

teller—a member of Congress who reads, records, and tallies up all the states' electoral votes following a presidential election

ticket—a political party's two candidates for president and vice president who run for election together

U.S. Constitution—the document that establishes the principles and laws of the United States government

To Find Out More

Books

Davis, Todd, and Marc E. Frey. *New Big Book of U.S. Presidents: A Young Reader's Guide to the Presidency*. Great Neck, NY: Oakwood Publishing, 1999.

Gutman, Dan. *Landslide! A Kid's Guide to the U.S. Elections*. New York: Aladdin Paperbacks, 2000.

Hewson, Martha S. *The Electoral College*. Philadelphia: Chelsea House Publishers, 2002.

Loomis, Burdett A., and Paul D. Schumaker, Editors. *Choosing a President: The Electoral College and Beyond*. New York: Chatham House Publishers, 2002.

Travis, Cathy. *The Constitution Translated for Kids*. Great Neck, NY: Oakwood Publishing, 2002.

Organizations and Online Sites

Federal Election Commission
http://www.fec.gov
This organization helps to monitor the financing of federal elections. It also provides a helpful section called "Elections and Voting" that includes information on the Electoral College and how it works.

How It Works
http://www.howitworks.com
This Web site is for young people and others who want to know more about a particular topic. It is a fun Web site that provides basic and easy-to-understand information to readers. There are sections on the site that describe how the Electoral College works, how Congress works, how elections work, and other political subjects.

National Archives
700 Pennsylvania Avenue, NW
Washington, D.C. 20408
http://www.nara.gov
If you want to see copies of the original Constitution, Bill of Rights, and other documents of national importance, this is

the site to check out. This site also includes the government's official Electoral College Web site.

The National League of Women Voters
1730 M Street, NW, Suite 1000
Washington, D.C. 20036-4508
http://www.lwv.org
This organization is committed to citizen involvement in elections, voting, and government affairs. Its Web site contains a wealth of information about U.S. election procedures, including the Electoral College.

Selected Supreme Court Decisions
http://supct.law.cornell.edu/supct/index.html
This site offers information about the Supreme Court's decision in the *Bush* v. *Gore* case, as well as general information about the Court and other decisions of interest.

The U.S. Congress
http://www.house.gov
http://www.senate.gov
Both the Senate and the House of Representatives have Web sites for young people. These sites provide a detailed look at the job of members of Congress and ways to contact senators and representatives. They also offer background information about the Constitution and other important historical documents and events.

A Note on Sources

To research this book, I read several books, numerous news articles, and Internet Web sites devoted to the subject. One book I found particularly helpful was *Securing Democracy: Why We Have an Electoral College*, edited by Gary L. Gregg II. It includes essays by renowned scholars, politicians, and political scientists that highlight different aspects of the Electoral College throughout U.S. history.

Written for a younger audience, Martha Hewson's *The Electoral College* offers an easy-to-read, accessible overview of the role the Electoral College plays in American elections. Finally, several books written about the controversial 2000 election brought the subject to life for me, especially *Supreme Injustice: How the High Court Hijacked the 2000 Election*, by Alan Dershowitz.

—*Suzanne LeVert*

Index

Numbers in *italics* indicate illustrations.

About the Author

Suzanne LeVert is the author of more than twenty nonfiction books for young readers, including several about the U.S. government. She is a graduate of New York University and Tulane Law School. She lives in New Orleans, Louisiana, where she is an assistant district attorney for Orleans Parish.